OUTLANDER

105 Selected Poems - And Additional Musings

LAWRENCE KLEPINGER

Order this book online at www.trafford.com
or email orders@trafford.com

Most Trafford titles are also available at major online book retailers.

Print information available on the last page.

ISBN: 978-1-4907-5637-0 (sc)
ISBN: 978-1-4907-5638-7 (hc)
ISBN: 978-1-4907-5639-4 (e)

Library of Congress Control Number: 2015903324

Trafford rev. 03/04/2015

 www.trafford.com
North America & international
toll-free: 1 888 232 4444 (USA & Canada)
fax: 812 355 4082

CONTENTS

LAWRENCE KLEPINGER

Discovering Lawrence Klepinger is like finding a mansion on a molehill. He has been described as a "writer's writer" in that he strives to express, in the most basic way, what is happening all around us.

Mr. Klepinger has been criticized for being too "negative" or an outright bitter person. These are the comments that usually accompany the man who chooses to tell the truth - in the most unpolished of terms - so as to discredit everything he has to say. It is the reaction of the insecure that act in such a manner.

You never hear epithets hurled at those who choose not to oppose the Status Quo, who only write in flowery "Pollyanna" type verse, or whose writing "offends" no one.

Having been raised in a lower income neighborhood, Mr. Klepinger understands, full well, the harsh rules of life.

When he was four years old he contracted polio, had the typical "arched back" but was able to completely recover.

At age 10, his first house was condemned by the State of California Highway Commission, by right of eminent domain. His father vowed never to have another home of his "stolen" by the government.

For the next five years, Lawrence and his father worked tirelessly to renovate an old house in Sylmar, California, located in yet another lower income neighborhood.

One evening, soon after his father came home from his junior high school teaching job, there was a knock on the door. His father answered, was quickly handed an envelope as the process server scurried away.

When his father started to read the notice, his hands began to shake, first with terror, then with unmitigated anger. He had just been served his second eviction notice, in the name of eminent domain, ironically for an extension of the same freeway that took his first house.

To this day, Lawrence Klepinger remembers his father slowly turning in the living room, an ashen color washing over his face, as he walked out to the backyard and began to cry. His father never recovered his spirit and slowly faded away, sank into alcohol, divorced his wife of 30 years and lived a broken existence from that point on.

After graduating from high school, Lawrence joined the Army and served 26 months, 11 days, in Vietnam, receiving the CIB, Purple Heart and various other service-connected awards. Having been wounded in the nose and eye with shrapnel, he was told that he might be blind in his right eye. Again, he made a full recovery.

Upon his return to America, he first attended El Camino College, in Gardena, California. During his first semester, while riding his brand new motorcycle, he was intentionally run off the road and almost killed. He was not wearing a helmet and flew in the air over 45 feet - and survived. However, his doctor told him he would walk with a limp. To the doctor's surprise, Mr. Klepinger again made a full recovery.

After graduating from El Camino, Mr. Klepinger transferred to San Jose State University, received a BA degree in political science, and an MA degree in education, sold real estate for two years, then worked for the City of San Jose for three years, before deciding to travel to Japan to pursue a fulltime English teaching career.

After retiring from teaching, he returned to America, ran for United States Congress in the state of Washington, and was narrowly defeated in the primary election of 2004.

In 2006 he was invited to teach English in China. Upon completion, he moved to Panama and was an educational consultant for eight months, before he and his wife, Akiko, decided to move back to Sacramento, to be near their children and grandchildren.

In 2014 he and his wife moved back to Japan and are currently living in Aomori Prefecture.

Mr. Klepinger has published textbooks by Barron's Educational Series, written a critically acclaimed novel entitled *LAND*, revolving around the aspects of a Vietnam Veteran's return "home" with an ending that has been raved about ever since its initial publication.

He is also the author of a non-fiction book laying bare the "real" goings-on in the People's Republic of China, entitled *CHINA HOUSE*, which almost got his passport revoked in the process, being warned that if he published it, while still living in China, there would indeed be "dire consequences."

He has published a series of maxims entitled, *MUSINGS*, which have gained widespread "cult" appeal for their pithy observations on life and living in general.

He has also published numerous newspaper features, academic articles that are still in use today, along with many political articles under the on-line blog entitled, *THE AMERICAN TELEGRAPH*.

With this short glimpse into Mr. Klepinger's background, it is not hard to realize why his poems have been read by many critical writers, numerous friends and colleagues, students both past and present, and the general reading public, all of whom, coming away with the same conclusion: Mr. Klepinger has a distinct style of writing, brutally honest in its approach, never backing away from a taboo subject, yet exceedingly poignant in its total scope and concept.

These poems run the full range of poetic style and creativity. Some are short, others funny in presentation, yet a number are dark and foreboding in their tone and maturity. Some rhyme, some are non-rhyming, while others simply ramble on to an always surprising conclusion.

Some poems will leave you nodding your head in agreement, yet at times, others will have you disagreeing vehemently in both word and content.

Yet, in the end, I guarantee you will find that Lawrence Klepinger is on to something that other people think about - but rarely take the time to express in writing - much less attach their name to.

Following each poem is a personal maxim, most of which are taken from Mr. Klepinger's books entitled *MUSINGS*, a series of eight books which he has written over the course of years.

These maxims are meant as a side-note and also a brief reprieve from reading one poem after another. Some are funny, some introspective, while others are given to commonsense concepts and ideas. Many of these maxims have been widely acclaimed as some of the best, and most witty sayings, of our time.

Sakon Maki
English Haiku and Senryu author

BRIEF PREFACE

Mr. Klepinger does not rely on one theme, nor does he adhere to a certain style of poetry writing. Some are rhyming, some unrhymed, while others abandon the constrictions of line count and rhyme altogether, choosing to let the poem make its own "natural breaks."

The concept of Political Correctness is refreshingly void in Lawrence Klepinger's poetry. At times, they seem rude – even crude. While in other instances, his style will run in total compliance with how poetry is "supposed" to be written.

With all this in mind, the reader will find not only enjoyment and inspiration but also a different angle on how to look at things in life from a totally unfamiliar perspective.

Finally, Mr. Klepinger's poems will, if nothing else, leave the reader with the feeling of experiencing a refreshingly new style of poetry – not Maudlin nor Panglossian – in his approach to writing.

Rather, the reader will come away with a definite sense of truth expressed in a uniquely poetic fashion.

Welcome to **OUTLANDER**.

OUTLANDER

.

I THOUGHT I KNEW IT ALL

Having just graduated from university
And received an honored degree,

The whole world opened wide
Waiting, just for me.

I'd change things that needed fixing
And speak truth at every turn,

Make the ignorant see my way
With the utmost of concern.

Yes, those ideas I had that day
As I beckoned to the call,

But so much had I yet to learn
When I thought I knew it all.

A hard-earned dollar isn't easily spent.

A SMILING SOLDIER

I had seen him around town
before he shipped out overseas,
talking casually with people in the bar,
hanging out in the coffee shop,
strolling through the grocery store,
laughing at stale jokes,
looking at young girls
admiring the medals on his chest.

Today he simply returned,
for a soldier who has gone to war
never really comes home.

He now has even more medals,
more stories he refuses to tell,
tightly bound into a shell
that only he knows
to be, the simple truth, left untold.

It's quiet in the room
and there is an aroma of tears,
but words that should be said
are left unspoken,
and as I turn around
one last time,
the sight I've seen
all too often,
a smiling soldier
sound asleep,
lying in a coffin.

In the end, public order will override
individual liberty.

A LITTLE BOY AND HIS DOG

I watched as
a little boy and his dog
walked down the pathway
in our local park,
conversing in a language
only they could understand.

Sometimes the boy would laugh
as the dog bounded ahead,
leaping over green hedges,
quickly circling maple trees,
chasing the occasional pigeon,
then stop abruptly
turn around and come back,

seemingly to encourage his friend
to continue thinking positive
as he struggled to keep his balance,
polio, aluminum crutches, hindering his
every, calculated step.

Yet, no matter how far ahead
the dog would run
he never failed to return,

making the little boy giggle,
again and again.

Two best friends are one too many.

IN THE FIRST PLACE

On this brief mortal span
we blithely refer to as life,
trespassing on the
tarmac of complacency,

puzzled by the conformity
of those who protest the loudest,
disinterested in the inherent
ever-present concept
of surviving another day,

I automatically plod on
through the darkness
of the familiar unknown,
searching for a reason
why I even do so,
unaware of the passage of time,
until it is too late,

then suddenly coming
to the numbing conclusion
that I finally made it through,
but had neglected to ever wake up
in time to live, in the first place.

Count on no one but yourself; then make sure to double-check your figures.

PRECIOUS PRIDE

Precious Pride
has been with me
as far back as I recall.
    Precious Pride
    has cushioned me
    from many a precarious fall.

Precious Pride
has saved my face
countless times in the past.
    Precious Pride,
    oh, what a disgrace
    when coming in dead last.

Precious Pride
kills more than guns
though few would dare agree.
    Precious Pride
    won't stand aside,
    for Love, nor Liberty!

Precious Pride
can sneak inside
all reason it can choke.
    For Precious Pride
    is nothing more
    than just a cruel joke.

You can win an argument and still be wrong.

A FOOL'S CONSORT

I have been stained
with the curse of mortality,

burdened to live
with the thought of dying,

never knowing for sure
when the hammer of darkness

will strike its harrowing blow
snuffing out the shadows of my dreams,

content with fruitless aspirations
temporarily stranded in a dimly lit hallway

connecting two dark rooms
void of doors and windows,

wrapped in silent mourning
forever lamenting not what has been accomplished,

rather, regretting lost opportunities
frittered away in consummate procrastination,

the fool's consort at the table
beckoning me to dine with halfwits

in accordance to the dictates of time,
as life's clock slowly winds down.

When you laugh at others you end up mocking yourself.

INTO THE VOID

From the mildewed manuscripts,
there is whispering
from the vanquished past,
in quiet undertones,
of that which should perish
and that which shall remain.

For in the chaos of the councils
in which fools ascribe to
the whims and wishes
of acrobats and magicians,
to the eternal glee
of the court jester
presiding over it all,

and to be intentionally written,
will obliterate the conscience of the soul
and forever extinguish that eternal light
emanating from the Grand Mansion,
that now sits atop of the hill.

When that time comes
from where will we get
the tallow to make candles
for the future,
and how shall we light them
once the fire is gone
from our souls?

A gun in the hands of a brave man is less dangerous than a knife in the hands of a coward.

BLIND SPOTS

Suckled on fear
bathed in solitary breathings
toweled by insecurity,

then set out on the road to success
does each man search in despair
through rummaging in the past
trying to reconcile the blind spots,

wondering if the stars stand still at night
realizing that they are present
even in the light of day,

but unable to perceive them
lacking the visionary power
to decipherer that which is

right before his very eyes,
yet still unable to see.

Unsolicited advice is best received when kept to yourself.

CRUMBS

The crumbs,
the issue of life
scattered before me,
unmitigated slaughter,
fraudulent claims
of peace and prosperity.

I bend and scrape,
trying to save
the meager bits
of what little remains,

a wound still bleeding
inflicted, centuries past,
post-mortem sweat
stinging the eyes of the dead,
in a never-ending conquest
of time that refuses to cease,

leaving those unlucky few who remain
to languish in the wilderness
least we have nowhere else to go
nothing left to subsist on,
vanquished hope, forever groping
the famine infested terrain.

Where on earth shall we find the dreams
with which to feed out children?

If you don't own the land then you are just renting.

OPINION OF AN EXPERT

On my way home from work today
I met a friend of mine who had majored
In botany when in college.

He was always eager to inform me
About every type of plant,
And their various species.

As we were walking along, I pointed
To an exquisite flower and commented
On its unique splendor.

My friend laughed, disdainfully,
Out of the corner of his mouth,
Informing me that it was only a weed.

Isn't it sad that sometimes
The education one is to live by
Rules out the beauty of life itself?

The arrogance of ignorance never ceases to amaze me.

CLOWNS

I don't know why
but clowns always
made me cry
deep down inside.

Their simple smile,
through doomsday paint
plastered on their faces,
seemed to be pleading for help
while pretending to laugh
at all of life's disgraces.

Yet for an instant
they always gave me
a peek, as a child,
what it felt like
to be funny,
to be free,
to be unfettered
by society's straightjacket
of jaundice pomp and fake civility.

And as I stumbled headlong
into the dreary onslaught of adulthood,
I remember their smile,
always trying to make me believe
that things really aren't all that bad,
yet, all the while,
smiling, ever smiling, so sad.

All life is speculation.

AND JUST LIKE THAT

And just like that
no more tomorrows,
yesterday's mistakes
vanish with the breath of time,

all thoughts of getting ahead
melt into thin air,
life insurance policy
now in effect,
gone forever
a flash in the pan,

nothing to look forward to
except the sunrise of eternity,
death in life
life in death,
one meaningless
without the other,
joyous songs of sorrow
laughing at the parade

no longer on the sidelines
now fully engaged,
in the book of short stories,
the final page.

Bestowing wisdom on a fool is akin to giving a lantern to a blind man.

PERPETUAL LONELINESS

In the end we are alone,
not in family or spiritual comfort,
but in real physical being,
we are in a constant state
of perpetual loneliness.

While driving in traffic,
in a crowded concert hall,
an overflowing restaurant,
we are all sitting in
a jam-packed stadium
observing the game of life
being played out,
in perpetual loneliness.

Lying in bed
your partner sound asleep,
as you ponder
what the next day will bring,
together in body
yet under the covers,
perpetual loneliness.

No one can escape it
not one of us
can run away,
no matter how hard we try,
we all live, and die,
in constant denial of,
perpetual loneliness.

A false sense of self-esteem will do more damage than true insight.

BE ON CONSTANT VIGIL

Be on constant vigil
for the vile, salubrious tongue.

Those vicious words,
uttered under the
penetrating guise
of eloquence personified,
so well-honed to such an extent
that those who are not
immediately taken asunder
are perceived as bigoted, racist,
self-centered, uncultured,
not caring, inhumane.

When, in fact,
as history has proven
time and again,
it is the gifted speaker
with such lubricous prose
that leads the naïve masses
to believe it is
in their best interests
to dig their own graves
with bare hands,
then back themselves up to the edge
and lift their arms up as they are
being eliminated en masse
for the benefit of society.

Be on constant vigil
for the vile, salubrious tongue.

Principles will hurt you, especially when they run counter to popular opinion.

DOGS AND CATS

While Dogs
are man's best friend,
and have
a stated purpose,

Cats,
in my opinion,
are nothing short
of worthless.

Learn to laugh at yourself; it makes life all the more fun.

HIGHER EDUCATION

Over the years,
As standards of
Academia have declined
To new heights,

An appropriate word will be
Invented to proclaim
When the time
To end all learning
Has finally arrived.

For, as the process
Of mental decay
Hastens up the incline,
And intelligence
chooses to succumb,

I venture they will call
That most hallowed of all
Establishments,
The Halls of Aka-dumb.

Being normal merely means that you have allowed yourself to be intimidated into submission by those around you.

HOLDING ON

I never took the time to notice
How much she had changed,

I was always busy elsewhere
Appointments rearranged.

I would drop by, time permitting,
Just to say hello,

Yet when I'd leave she'd always smile,
But wished I wouldn't go.

Sometimes we'd talk, just to talk,
But nothing much was said,

She'd pretend to understand
And gently nod her head.

Now sitting here beside her
Hand in hand since dawn,

My mother died this morning
But I'm still holding on.

The writing on the wall is of little use,
if you can't read.

INTO BONDAGE

Into bondage
does the common man stumble,

forced not by the loathing
of some despotic dictator,

but by the gentle persuasion
of logical tradition,

the collaboration of the few
confounded by the ignorance of the many,

intelligence sublime
pretending to have all the answers,

the humble acquiesce
of stupidity personified,

a quorum of the ill-informed
leading the quandary of the masses

into a prison in which
all is taken care of,

save the sanctity
of the Sovereign Individual.

To control how people speak is the first step in dictating how they will think.

LASCIVIOUS LICENSE

Lavishly languid,
Lightning lurks,

Leaving lyrics,
Laughingly limpid,

Learning later,
Luxury lost,

Lamenting loosely
Logical lust,

Living ludicrous
Liquor lies,

Lifting lesser,
Lowdown lives.

It is not wise to confuse facts with the truth.

PARCHED FIELDS

I reached the parched fields
in time to witness the carnage
that had taken place
just a few days before.

Thousands of bodies
lying in contorted forms,
brown and rusting,

red waves
of blood-colored hue,
etched in
the fading background.

The essence of
a past season,
yet the promise
of better days to come,

autumn time,
raking leaves
in the early morning sun.

The passion for acceptance is the most destructive endeavor in the human experience.

TOMORROW

If, in time of despair,
the conscience of discontent
needles its elbow into your side,
laughs at your plight and snickers
at the predicament you are in,

set your sails to the winds
of the future, and dwell on
nothing but the success
of positive thinking.

Leave those, who so tenaciously
cling to failure like a lost lover from the past,
to wallow in their grief,

while you shake off
the momentary loss of the present,
and dwell on the goal of success,
that only tomorrow has to offer.

It is better to define yourself according to your own dictates, rather than adhere to the wishes of others.

TRANQUILITY OF LIFE

To ensure tranquility of life,
say nothing to offend anybody,

keep to the middle of the road
question not, least you be ridiculed,

pose no threat to tyrants,
pretend to be happy, even if you aren't

always extend a glad hand
especially to those who don't deserve it,

accept things just as they are
and above all, get used to it.

Do this and I guarantee you will have a
peaceful, tranquil existence,

and when you die, your life will have been
totally, and completely, good for nothing at all.

In silent reticence does the average man quiver and shake at the prospect of having to get involved.

UNMATCHED CHOPSTICKS

The confusion of life
spills out before my eyes
like a mystic spreads his obligatory fortune straws
on the ground, then picking them up
one by one, deciphering what they represent,

a jumbled grasping with assumed guesses,
a confusion of light and dark meanings,
never comprehending the difference
between fate and destiny,

a mind riddled with the attendant oxymoron
laughing at my bewilderment,
constantly beckoning me to see if I can
remediate the consequent purpose
of my existence, seemingly as easy
as plucking raindrops
in a torrential downpour
with a pair of unmatched chopsticks.

Gently lead your opponents into a trap; never force them.

VENGEANCE

Vengeance is a cancer
That clings to my soul,
I try to cut it out of me
But yet, it won't let go.

I see it fester in others
And realize the power of hate,
Yet I have fed it so many times
It's become my soulmate.

Vitriol is its mainstay
Of which I freely consume,
If I don't change the way I live
Vengeance, will be my doom.

To sow the seeds of revenge is the most fruitless of undertakings.

SHORT-TIME

Avenues on fire
night lights burning bright
slutty whores sell
their well-worn wares
to drunken servicemen,

ulcerated vaginas
the county fair,
ten bucks a ride
wounding the innocent
along with the guilty
collateral damage gone awry,

praying God isn't looking,
sweaty and grappling
rancid sperm
infecting everything it touches.

Mothers taking on boys
young enough to be their sons
supine on filthy, alley mattresses,
like an organ-grinder
with a chained monkey
a tin cup full of copper pennies,

enticing prospective customers
to purchase sex
for a short-time,
love not included.

When innocence is extinguished, survival sets the table.

WHAT HAS BECOME

What has become already is,
a harbinger of that which will follow,

a confused litany of prescribed emotions,
none of which are real, yet forever present nonetheless,

earmarked by the ages, soothed by indiscriminate withdrawal,
coaxed on by a false sense of reality, never to give up,
fully aware that life, as we know it, is a lighthearted farce.

From the first moment we draw breath, starting to cry,
as we never did in our mother's womb,

a grave error, we gently plod on, an exit to the beginning,
a blank headstone resting, silent on our tomb,
save the worms cultivating the cemetery soil.

Life expectancy has nothing to do with the expectations of life.

WE LEARN TO BEHAVE

Like rats in a daze,
we run through the maze
of life and its social constrictions.

Pretending we know
which way to go
drugged up on legal prescriptions.

With roads well-paved
we learn to behave
adhering to pre-set convictions.

We claim to be free
but how can that be,
when all we have are restrictions?

Conscience is the first arbiter of self-discipline.

WOUNDED HOUSE

I abide in a wounded house
incessantly coerced
with enduring fear,

my fulltime occupation
to endure
until the following day,

my ears packed full
of ubiquitous promises
my belly growls for lack of nourishment,

my brain on a murder spree
ransacking everything
inside my head,

aching to be free
the very second
I am dead.

If ambition outweighs ability, frustration prevails.

YOUTH

Take not youth
eternally,

for in a lightening flash
it will vanish,

leaving all those
left standing
obliterated in shock,

stuttering and stammering,
trying to make sense
of what just happened,

groping in the
ever-dawning darkness,

desperately trying to evade
that menacing shadow
clinging so tenaciously
to that form that once was,

the youthful body
of beauty,
spiced with love and lust,

now slowly rushing
to return to dust.

What you perceive in life depends upon the way you look at things.

A FRIEND

Be you truthful
With a friend

And lose his friendship
In the end,

Be not angry
Nor be sad,

You lost a friend
You never had.

The insecure man will always misinterpret constructive criticism as an affront to his dignity.

NEW YEAR'S RESOLUTION

I am afflicted by HDD, High Dilatory Disease,
a medical condition that affects everything I don't do.

The "classic" car taking up space in my back yard,
a trestle for weeds, that I will restore someday,
the unfinished novel in the bottom drawer
of my desk, yet to be completed,
the scribbles of poems that I have not fully
organized, let alone revised,
the family photo album that I have attempted
to redo, on any number of occasions,

the Spanish language book I have opened a hundred times,
but never gotten past chapter two,
the guitar I promised myself that I would learn to play,
gathering dust in the corner of my living room.

The friends I promised to call, the letters I haven't written,
the physical examination I have, as yet, to make,
my last will and testament, still not drawn up,
and a slew of other chores I have continually put off.

But today, I will vow to turn over a new leaf,
make a New Year's Resolution to do all of the above
without excuse or hesitation, to finally get them all done,
and be free of the yoke that they have placed around my neck,

just as soon as I have another donut,
and one more cup of coffee.

The hardest part about painting a house lies in the preparation.

CANNIBALIZE OUR YOUNG

We are the ones
who cannibalize our young,

putting them into
situations that can't be won,

crowding at the trough
we slurp and suck,

while keeping our young
far from the cup.

What's mine is mine
to hell with the future,

with a hand like a surgeon
we clip every suture.

And low and behold
as our young advance,

they deny the old
as if in a trance.

And then they too
will consume their young,

for as they are taught
so will it be done.

When need succumbs to greed, you bleed.

DAILY ROBOTIC PLEDGE

Very rarely
do I vary
from the cast
that I've been mold,

the song I sing
will be with me
from now
until I'm old.

While trying to reach
a crimson ring
of which I am to hold,

I weave a pattern
of my life
with colors drab and cold.

Yet very rarely varying
the time that I have sold,
not doing what I want to do,
but rather, as I'm told.

If you always seek the middle of the road you will have no say in the direction it takes.

GROWN UP

You know you have
grown up
when you return
to your hometown
and everything
seems much smaller.

It is only then
that you realize
how minute
your childhood
really was,
how insignificant
your existence
actually is,

yet how
supremely important
it all seemed
at the time.

Adhering to a religious preference is like having a favorite baseball team; it usually depends upon where you are from.

HIS FINAL SUIT

His passion for diamonds,
lust for gold, the richest man in town,
money by the buckets-full
no longer stacking gold coins.

A life of warlike conquest
wrapped around his soul
like a hangman's noose,
now lying in state
for all to see.

The silk, black outfit,
exquisitely tailored,
white carnation
pinned to his lapel,
every button
in perfect order,
purple eyes
in recessed sockets,
his final suit
that has no pockets.

A profit margin is the difference between what you pay for something and what it is actually worth.

KEYSTROKES

There!
That should do it.
Now just a little cut and paste,
press this key and . . .

Finally done.
Short story completed.

What! What happened?
Where did that paragraph go?
Undo cut.

What the hell? That's not right.
Better type the whole paragraph over.
Don't want to screw it up
anymore than it already is.

Now how did it go?
Damn it. Can't remember.
Wonder if I could re-retrieve it?
Press undo paste and . . .
Where did that come from?

Son-of-a-bitch,
this is not a computer,
it is just a pile of shit
with knobs on it.

You foul up this story
any further
and I'll throw your ass
off the balcony.

Now, I'll press and re-type it and . . .
What! That's it.
I have had it with you.

Back to my typewriter.
Never should have bought
a damn computer in the first place.

At least, with my typewriter
I know what I am writing
won't be eaten up
by some stupid machine.

Never should have quit using it
in the first place.
If it was good enough
for Hemingway,
then it sure as hell is
good enough for me.

Easy to set up,
no plugging in,
no gadgets to fiddle with,
slip in a piece of paper
and presto.

What the . . .

No typewriter ribbon!

When I was young all I had to do was catch on; now that I am older, all I try to do is catch up.

ROAD SIGNS

The journey is not easy street,
rather a parade of terrifying simplicity,
nor is a roadmap issued before the trip.

At the beginning it is twisted
beyond comprehension,
a change of direction, not planned,
ups and downs, then up again
trying to negotiate those on all sides.

TOLL BRIDGE AHEAD, dig for more money.

Then an unforeseen pothole
an unexpected,

DETOUR!
NO U-TURN!
SLIPPERY WHEN WET!

Now, headed back to the straight and narrow,
only to swerve off course while daydreaming,
hitting wake-up bumps on the shoulder,
narrowly missing the guardrail
haphazardly placed where least expected,

just ahead of the RUNAWAY PIT,
filled to the brim with soft sand,
bent on inflicting a hellacious,
neck-jarring stop.

Then on to the next FREEWAY,
existence floor-boarded
in the general direction of perceived success.

MERGING TRAFFIC!
YIELD!
DO NOT PASS!

Look out!

ROUNDABOUT!
UNCONTROLLED INTERSECTION!
SLOW DOWN!

Watch out!

DO NOT ENTER!
WRONG WAY!
STOP!

Finally, a light at the end of the tunnel
only to be disappointed,
totally confused and frustrated,

silently submitting to
the relentless realization
that, sooner or later, all roads lead to a

DEAD END.

Give people the choice between chaos and dictatorship and they will opt for the latter every time.

APATHY

Apathy is the only thing
That has buried men,

It beckons an inactive state
And destroys them from within,

It never puts itself in view,
But lurks behind a grin,

Enticing each and everyone
Not to try again.

It is truly the disadvantaged man who thinks himself so.

BRIGHT-EYED CHILDREN

Oh,
what a wicked
lesson's in store,

when
bright-eyed children
march off to war.

It is the solemn duty of the true patriot to chastise those wrongful elements of the country he so loves.

BY THE HEARTHSTONE

The kiss of springtime
marks the end of winter,
sending forth a new year.

The breathless hush
a forbidden embrace
trembling fingers,
an errant tear
a love song in eternity
so far, yet so near.

Another summer
will repeat again,
and fall will see
the leaves on fire
that light the way
to another winter,

as we huddle
by the hearthstone
of our birthright,
watching life go by.

All life is compromise.

CONTINUE TO ROW

I see no one around me
though I'm standing in a crowd,

it would be very interesting
if I began to scream out loud.

Then again, they would ignore me
their eyes as desolate as the moon

expressionless are the faces
the same at midnight, as at noon.

The guile of the masses
like passing ships in the night,

devoid of any contact
in desperation, they take flight.

Yet, I keep on going
upstream against the flow,

I'm on the outside, looking out
But yet, continue to row.

Every society exists at the expense of the Sovereign Individual.

IN STEP WITH THE MOON

Dancing in the sunshine
Clamoring in shadows,

The mist of past memories
Evaporating with time,

Succulent promises gone awry
Advancing, but making no progress.

The ocean moves
In step with the moon

As I talk in serious tones
To myself, and answer.

I was going to
Change the world,

But instead, the world
Changed me.

Honesty is such an inexpensive commodity, yet few people choose to buy it.

INHERITANCE

The sisters
I never knew,

in a festive mood
came smiling

to my mother's funeral,
the splendor of

pious concern
pursuing their every move

with the foul stench
of inheritance,

in the shadow
of their wake.

A spider does not have to be told how
to spin its own web.

ISN'T IT IRONIC

Isn't it ironic how suicide
and pride live side by side,
yet refuse to admit
in the same house abide,

smarting at insults, recoiling, a chide,
the chauffer of culture a drunken guide,
groping for cover in which to hide,

scorning compassion afraid to confide,
fragments of past lives daily collide,
where truth was a cancer and intercourse lied,
the conscience of innocence upon which it spied,
beckoned like friendship to take a short ride,

and promise forever to stand by your side,
yet finally retreating on the outgoing tide.

With courage and temper raging inside
killing each other, who knows who died.

Isn't it ironic,
how suicide survived.

Suicide: The ultimate form of social protest.

KNOWLEDGE

Only those
who yearn to learn

will enlightened
knowledge surely burn,

but they are few
and far between,

for idiots rule
the world supreme.

The advancement of man will not annihilate us; only his ignorance can accomplish that task.

I KNOW PEOPLE

I know people
who want to impress,

they adopt a way of acting
and a different mode of dress,

to them being noticed
is the name of the game,

but when they get together
they all look just the same.

If you are always worried about fitting in, you will never stand out.

LIGHTHOUSE

In the dark
a lighthouse
is moaning
its warning signal,

then flashes danger
on the surrounding
rocks below,

steer clear
of this area,
or else
risk running aground,
and sinking.

If I had only
paid attention
when my parents
were speaking,

I'd be so much
better off today.

Men profess the virtues of their ancestors as if honor and dignity were hereditary.

LOOK AT ME

Everyone is selling Me,
selling all the time.

The self-promotion
fantasy idol,
Me Incorporated,
a legend in my own mind.

Brand Me,
Copy Me,
Believe Me,

Self-esteem,
What does that word mean?

Look at Me,
there is no one else
in this world,
but Me.

Not, Me, Myself and I.
It is just Me, Me, Me.

Why can't anyone else see
The only one really important,
is Me.

Mommy, Daddy,
Look at Me!

A fool is his own most captive
audience.

LOOSE ENDS

What are these threads
that keep tugging at my mind,
the ones that I am still bound by?

They entangle me
like an unmercifully bad dream,
yet are not nightmares,
merely threads of the past
that keep pestering me
for some kind of recognition,
final retribution, if you will.

Sometimes I find a thread or two
when I am not even looking,
surprised, by a certain scent,
an innocently uttered phrase,
a song that had long since, slipped into the past.

Save, for those certain threads,
that jostle me out of my daily trance,
and reassure me that the threads of my past,
are what I am made of, woven into who I am
reminding me where I once was,
why I am going in the direction that I am,
trying to thread the eye of a needle so that I may finally
sew up the matters that still remain,
yet, constantly forgetting
to lick the frayed end so as to fit it through
the glare of that final curtain call,
life coming to a close,
time to tie up loose ends.

Never put off until tomorrow what should have been done yesterday.

MAN, TO LOVE

What feeble attempt
man, to love.

As though giving alms
to a mournful beggar,

adept in his misfortune
the proclamation
of all religions
to give a tithing,

thus reliving
the burden of guilt,

while pocketing
the other nine-tenths
for ourselves.

What feeble attempt
man, to love.

To disobey a bad order is much more heroic than to obey a good one.

MANICURED CHAOS

In the confusion
of lost ways

the pallbearers of
paranoid suspicion

will cast their net
of manicured chaos.

For in that confusion
will the tyrant find solitude

while garnering more power
to repress the people

until they have had enough,
rebuke the tyrant,

and feverishly retain another
to take his place,

a different manner, an unknown face
but all in all, one just as base.

The government is never to be blamed for anything; in every instance, the people are to be held responsible.

MY MIRROR

For the first time in a long time,
I stood in front of my mirror,
and saw myself squinting back at me.

But there were too many wrinkles,
birds-feet scratched
at the corner of my eyes,

my nose was too red,
probably from
excessive drinking,

and my hair had begun to fall out,
brown age marks
pocked my forehead.

Suddenly I began
to feel sick.

It was then
that I understood
why there is
a medicine cabinet,
located just behind
my mirror.

Getting old is not for everyone.

NO COINCIDENCE

Life, and living,
is no coincidence.
It happens by design
not from the outside,
but from within.

Never allow
others to preach
who you are
or where you
should be going.

Freedom of choice
is your most powerful weapon,
hold it close to your chest,
hone the blade of individuality
to a virtuous edge.

Avenge not those
who have done you wrong,
but prove to them
that it was they
who committed the illicit act.

Fear not those who will
rise up and speak against you,
there will be many,
for there is no greater calamity
to the Status Quo,
than that of unbridled truth.

And, if your heart is without guilt,
you will be the receiver
of generous requital,
yet in your hour of glory
make not a move to gloat
nor a pretense of arrogance,

for that is to be left to lesser men,
those who strain to look up to you
for having the courage and wisdom
they so jealously covet,
but will never enjoy.

With peace in your heart,
yet strength in your soul
honesty will, in the end,
be your strongest shield.

Never submit to the forces of evil,
always strive for what you feel is right,
but bear in mind that with freedom
comes even a greater amount
of personal responsibility,

not only to those around you,
but also to yourself,
remain true,

and all your days will be filled
with joyous rapture,
the likes of which
only an honest man can
truly afford to endure.

Sometimes the ability to think freely can be a prison unto itself.

NO PETS ALLOWED

The small dog,
scraggly and undernourished,
kept staring at me in the rain,
I knew what he wanted.
I walked faster,
heading for my apartment,
glancing briefly at the sign
posted at the entrance:

NO PETS ALLOWED

I tried to console myself
that if it were OK to have a pet,
I'd bring him in out of the rain.

But I wondered if that was
the truth, or just an excuse.
I walked inside and closed the door,
leaving him sitting
at the edge of the sidewalk.

Minutes later I peeked out
to see if he was still there.
He was nowhere in sight,
but now firmly housed
inside my conscience,
a constant reminder
of the hypocrite,
I really am.

Daily we walk a razor-thin line between respectability and complete debauchery; it all depends upon who is watching.

NOT A GIVEN

I suffer from not knowing
who I am, frightened by what I
believe to be true,
yet lacking all means
of substantial verification
as to what is, and what is not.

I stumble along clawing at the air,
knowing it is there but still can't see it,
the secret faith of believing
something you cannot observe,
like passionate love, morbid hate,
always present, yet invisible.

To what strings are the stars attached?
Is it possible to draw back the curtain of the universe?
The veins in an autumn leaf, did they not bleed when it fell?

How am I to know where to walk,
what to do when I get there
as if trying to tell what time it is
on the dark side of the moon,
or in acknowledging that the precise hour
had any relevance to the present,
knowing fair well that yesterday is of the past,
this is the here, the now, but also, shackled
with the nagging realization that, no matter what
the circumstances may actually be,
tomorrow is not a given.

Death is nothing more than an exit to
the beginning.

THE KING: ON PONDERING
THE YOUNG PETITION

"These youth who protest
Know not how good they have it.
Why, when I was their age
I broke my back for a mere copper cent.
Instead of spending time to evaluate
The system which gave them birth,
They incite riots and throw rocks
Not realizing the Nation's true worth.

They say the establishment has refused
The most wholesome laws for the public good.
They say we have blackmailed our governors
To not pass laws of immediate and pressing importance.
Why, they say we have refused to pass other laws
For the accommodations of large districts of people.
If these people want further accommodations
For their cities inhabitants,
This shall be done, through the system alone,
For an unqualified handout
This government will never condone!

These young people state that
We have broken up demonstrations
By the representatives of the populace.
They claim this to be,
An invasion on the rights of the people.
They say we have not recognized
Their duly elected officials.
They even complain about arbitrary protection
Of our existing police force,
Claiming possible convulsions from within.
These young, ignorant, pseudo intellectuals
Claim to want more people of different race

Intermingled in their City State.
Do you realize how foolish
They really are?
You and I know
They'll not get very far!
But let us read further
With amusing delight,
And find out what else
They think is not right.

Why look, they say we've obscured justice
And made judges dependant on our will alone.
They say bureaucracies are excess in size,
And that during times of peace
We have standing armies among them.
They contend that the military machine
Is superior, not subordinate to, the peoples' will.
They say we protect our servicemen
By a mock trial, from punishment
For any murders which they should commit
On the inhabitants of these States.
They complain of no benefit of trial by jury.
They say we have taken away their freedom,
Torn up their charters, and wage war against them.
They say the establishment
Has plundered their seas, ravaged their coasts
And destroyed the lives of their people.
They say the populace is conscripted
To fight on the wrong side of right.

Listen how foolish it is,
If I may bequeath upon you a partial quote,
        'In every stage of these oppressions
        We have petitioned for redress
        In the most humble terms;
        Our repeated petitions have been answered
        Only by repeated injury.'

They are now taking it upon themselves
To insure freedom and justice for all.
They claim that they have
Certain unalienable rights, of which are,
    Life,
        Liberty,
            And the
                Pursuit of Happiness.
How foolish and insubordinate
Can these young upstarts be?
They don't realize that this
Establishment was founded on liberty!
We must now banish these views
With our armies of men,
To stop these ideas,
Before they begin!
For our wealth and status
Are gone with revolution,
We must devise a plan
For their ultimate execution.

An end to this nonsense and foolish pride,
We know we're right, down deep inside!
But before we suppress this childish talk,
I forgot to ask,
    Who is John Hancock?"

It is much more desirable that a government fear its people, rather than the other way around.

THE ONE THAT GOT AWAY

I learned young
to work hard and save,
not to let money burn
a hole in my pocket,

kept heading toward the future
with a jaundice eye on the past,
was frugal, yet not stingy,
paid off the mortgage,

cash for everything else
never absent, nor late for work,
my nose to the grindstone
with early retirement on the horizon,

my fly rod waiting in the corner
for that fateful day,
then, the final handshakes
goodbye to my co-workers,

now sitting in my boat,
casting overhead, I remember what they said,
"I never thought he'd make it,
he'll work 'til his dying day."

Reaching for a cold can of beer
fly dancing on the water,
smiling to myself,
the one that got away.

The concept of fate is folly, a social contrivance to keep men in their place and meekly accept their lot in life.

OUT THERE

Out there,
Horrible things are taking place,
Lying, cheating, stealing,

Clothed in the veil of false religions
       Lapping up our children's blood.

Out there,
Millions of people are dying,
     Hunger, famine, disease,
       They are eating our children.
      I don't want to see them,
         To face reality.

Out there,
Terrible things are happening,
     Murder, rape, pillage going on,
         And on,
           And on . . . .
In here,
A peaceful box,
Safe, warm, secure, comfortable.

I'm afraid of the future.
     What's waiting,
         Out There.

If good men refuse to get involved in politics, charlatans will do so in their own behalf.

THAT PENSIVE LOOK

I find it endlessly amusing
how poets, when being photographed,
like to assume that pensive look,
striking a pose of intellectual authority,

index finger positioned
deftly on the right cheek
not smiling for the camera,

pretending to see
what others are too ignorant
to fully comprehend,

as though they have
some sort of inside information
as to what life is all about,

when, in fact, they don't know
any more than anybody else
as to what the hell
is really going on.

Arrogance is the common denominator of insecure men.

SWIMMING IN THE EMPTINESS

I am one,
swimming in the emptiness
of a sea of people,
blank faces staring
at nothingness,
pretending to smile
with a scorn as deep
as the Grand Canyon,

lovingly giving
to the local charity,
eager to claim a tax write-off
piously proclaiming their willingness
to help the less fortunate,
while all the time
cursing them for their status in life,
giving no second thought
as to how lucky they are
not to be one in their company.

Swimming in the emptiness,
drowning in a
syrup of hypocrisy,
gasping for air,
suffocating in futility,
no longer swimming,
simply treading life
as it presents itself,
slowly closing my eyes.

In the wilderness all matter is tame;
it is in civilization that wild animals
lurk.

THE ARROGANCE OF IGNORANCE

The arrogance of ignorance
his righteous eyes ablaze,

indignant at his mishandling
by society's maze,

spewing forth his
self-proclaimed innocence
white froth foaming
at the corners of his mouth,

an epileptic seizure
unable to extinguish
the all-consuming hate,

blaming the consequences
of unbridled fate,

hurling epithets at all those
he holds responsible
for his failure in life,

trying desperately
to deflect the blame
pointing an accusing finger
at everyone within sight,

except back at himself
where the root of the problem
ultimately lies.

Fact and fiction are only separated by the will to believe; logic has no bearing on the matter.

THE ABANDONMENT

On the day of final atonement
the abandonment took place with scarcely a peep.

Commonsense was replaced by those who "just knew"
what was considered to be correct.

All the different people were placed in an identical room,
language was verboten, everyone simply began to mutter.

Memory came apart and therefore
no more learning was deemed appropriate.

Most lethal laws were the ones unwritten, adhered to
by the vast majority in the collectivity of the few.

Doors were no longer needed, all windows to the outside
were painted black with purple trim.

The corridors were permanently lined with two-way mirrors that
showed only one side of the spectrum.

The council of habitual knaves, wagging their tongues
and pointing fingers, a collection of licensed bullies,
blaming past discrepancies on dead bodies,
whose lips have turned to worms of vomit
now incapable of defending themselves,

forever detained in agitated purgatory
for declining to even put up a good fight
when the appropriate time presented itself.

Man is the only animal on earth that,
by choice, is not free.

the progress of man

the constant change
of things staying the same

the impermanence
of ever-present stability

the status quo
of endless revolutions

the past meticulously
deconstructed by the present

the familiar forever in flux
to make way for future retardation

leading to the synthetic compromise
of mental malnutrition

blithely referred to as
the progress of man

ignorance seeks council among its own

NO MORE SHADOWS

Fate offers no security
as destiny engulfs me
with the essence
of my final hour,

the passing of
life's invincible,
pallid remnants
of the man
I used to be,

as I amuse myself
with a tepid thought,

wondering if where
I am going
there will be
no more shadows,
following me.

Consensus of the mind will produce cognizance of the soul.

ONLY THE PRETTY

Only the pretty
are expected to achieve,
the ugly among us
are conditioned to believe,

youthful charm
the pedigree
only people of lesser looks
would dare disagree.

But for those who wallow
in such hideous apparel
adhering to comic logic
deceived by social betrayal,

as a blood sport
choreographed abuse
starved for compassion
from early youth,

I pity, but don't hate, you
for the life that you lead,
the scars you've collected
forbid you to bleed,

for through it all
you continually miss,
the blanket called love,
and a comforting kiss.

Lies depend on truth not being substantiated.

OPENING OLD WOUNDS

Echoes of taunting laughter
raw, vulnerable, whispering in my ear
reminiscent of the foggy past
as if it just happened yesterday,
faded photographs, yellow and crinkled,
chipped at the edges like an antique, porcelain tea cup.

Getting old, the dreadful disease
that will plague us all, save those lucky enough
to die before getting there.

Beautiful flesh, now gaunt and wrinkled,
delight, a lost concept buried in an old shoebox
of dog-eared baseball cards, a high school ring never worn,
my first love dead and gone, as are the past memories,
no more use lingering on.

The house I lived in, forever condemned
a new freeway took it away, a class reunion unattended
the familiar stomping ground, now distant and foreboding,
no longer where I grew up, just a phantasm of what I thought real
gone forever, maybe it never was.
Opening old wounds,
the puss of the past, airing out dirty laundry.

I breathe deep,
roll up my car window,
and drive through my hometown
as fast as I can.

Home is not where you were born, nor where you are from: Home is where you feel you belong.

THE GENTLE WAR

It began with the usual sigh,
buttons were pushed
soldiers sitting at their desks,
row upon row, charting, locating, zeroing in on
a myriad of designated targets for the day.

The animated blasts on computer screens,
direct hit, the occasional miss
a school here, a hospital there
no one seemed to really care,
it was actually pretty fun.

These gentle warriors
know not the sound of
a panicked baby crying
in its dead mother's arms,
the rancid smell of human flesh burning
a pretty, young girl's severed head
lying in the street, still smiling.

Accepted atrocities, legal genocide
by authoritative decree,
killing in the name of God,
for the love of it all.

No burning embers,
no charred ruins of naked corpses,
no buckets of blood, no shredded bodies,
no scent of the aftermath
the cyclone death from above,
the black, gleaming mouth
of the war dragon, consuming all in its path.
Again, the gentle press
of the button, precise annihilation,

no splattered intestines
no soft, grey brains
no piss in the pants
no uncontrolled bowels
no screams
no pleas for help
no time to think
no more trampled bodies
no more living, just the dead.

Coordinated holocaust, for a just cause
for the security of the country,
for the good of the people
the perpetuation of peace.

The automated cleanliness,
the antiseptic odor
coming from the restroom,
interspersed among the savory accent
of freshly brewed coffee,
cream and sugar upon request,
if you ask, they will even bring it
to your desk.

And the Gentle War rages on.

There has never been a war that has not been fought in the name of peace.

THE HALLWAY

The hallway
holds past memories
clogging the heart,

weighing down the spirit to move,
forever unwilling to sweep away
the accumulated clutter of years,
constantly threatening to do so,

in need of a total spring cleaning,
but reluctant to let go of the past,
notches on the door jamb
measuring the growth of children,

like family portraits adorning the hallway
of an era gone by, no longer relevant
yet forever there just the same.

It is easy to live in a house, once it is built.

THE HARROWING LIFE

The harrowing life
born of tortured blood,
dragged out of the womb
of warmth and comfort
with no recollection
of what it really felt like,

but a recalled existence
of a motion in sanguinity
ruptured by the time of exit,
from birth, through life,
a passage of trial and error,

tempered in turmoil
taunted in perspective
tempted in pervasiveness,

living in a nightmare of doubt,
screaming in silence
to find a way out.

You are born with your own unique set of ingredients; how you apply them determines your recipe for life.

YOUTH AND TRUTH

Youth and truth
appear to rhyme,

but tend to fade
with the passage of time.

Just because we get older is no guarantee
we get any wiser.

I WONDER

Granted,
Alcohol is a poison,

But I wonder which is worse,
To live a life of debauchery,

Or simply,
Die of thirst?

I never drink in the AM, unless I start in the PM.

148

MARRIED LIFE VS. SINGLE LIFE

Married life
Is rife with strife
Concussions, and debris,

Conscientious deliberations
Of how it ought to be.

Single life is
Much the same
Or so it seems to me,

Catacombs of endless choices
Pretending to be free.

Isn't it ironic that there is only one letter separating the word marriage from mirage?

OH, BUT FOR THE LACK
OF COURAGE

Oh, but for the lack of courage,
what could I have accomplished.

I just played a part and pretended that I didn't see
the maddening injustice that surrounded me,
every step I took on my insignificant path of life.

Indifference is as much the seed of cowardice,
as is inspiration that lacks the continence of action.

For therein lies the folly of future generations,
entwined in the travesty of individual men
who choose to succumb to the vicar of passion,

consorting with the benign creator of jealous greed,
the concubine of freedom, willingly forced into
consensual intercourse of a naïve mind,

while firmly pressed upon the altar
of the dictates of society,
entrenched in a stolid quagmire
that knows nothing but intrigue,
meddling confusion and petty hatred,
composed in a soliloquy of passion
that somehow passes the test of time.

Oh, but for the lack of courage,
what could I have accomplished!

Your principles should never be subject to arbitration.

MISSING PARTS

We begin with a jigsaw puzzle, instructions not included.
You start with a mess, then try to assemble everything
in the proper order.

On occasion, the pieces work fine
and snap into place, while other times
it takes forever to find the right fit,
trying one piece, then another, and after awhile
giving up altogether, and moving to a different
area, working on that for the time being.

Then, when everything starts to take shape, you return to the spot
that was giving you trouble, find the precise piece that matches,
hook all the sections together, then sit back and marvel
at how you finally made everything work out.

But the most depressing thing about such an undertaking,
is getting to the end, and finding out that one piece is not there,

a personal letter that went unanswered,
betrayal of a best friend,
an undeserved public rebuke
the mortal sting of a tarnished love affair,
a missed promotion, lost job
promises broken, debts not repaid,
yet, still satisfied at trying
to make it all work out,
happy at the overall outcome
of giving it your best shot,
missing parts and all.

Shoot for the stars – settle for the moon.

LANGUISHING

Languishing in the present I find myself
longing for the past, knowing all too well
it is gone, never to come again.

The niceties of being polite,
friendly smiles on the street,
honesty as a way of life,
your word as good as your bond.

Despite the termites of civility
constantly gnawing at the foundation
of our present being,

I continue to plod in the direction
of the future, wherever that may be,
teaching my children that good seeds
produce better fruit, instilling in them
a love and respect toward others,

but above all a concept that,
even in the darkest of times,
a negative outlook leads to more
depression and despair.

In the final analysis only the light
of a positive frame of reference
will shine through, to brighten a future
that, at times, refuses to offer any hope at all,
for those still languishing.

Don't try to change the whole world
for the better - just a small part of it.

FOR THE MAKING

The door
is right there in front of you,

the helping hand
is located on
the lower portion
of your right arm.

Reach out, turn the knob,
open your own door
to opportunity,

and be on your way
to gaining the status of
being your own man

by helping yourself
to the future.

Your life is yours,
for the making.

One termite can befall a castle.

FROM AFAR

Standing in the evening dusk
I watch the stars meekly peer out
from the darkening sky,

some smiling, some frowning,
others simply wandering by.

I find myself gazing up
not knowing what I see,

but realizing that I am looking at something
I can't explain, yet it somehow speaks to me.

But there it is, and thus,
I stare, wondering if
someone else is doing the same
on a planet,
a different plane,

and we on Earth
are nothing
but a star,
dangling
in their universe,
from afar.

A sad sight indeed, to see a man with two good eyes, but lacking any vision.

GONE, FOREVERMORE

Destruction
is the fate of man
in the purest
form of gloom,

yet he breaks
the sod of Earth
in which the flowers bloom.

But once
the fragrant blossoms shed
gone, forevermore,

they gently fall
on soldier's graves,
they're gone,
but not so, war.

Arms manufacturers make a killing.

GOOD HEALTH

We take our health for granted
Strong legs that help us stand,

Yet suddenly, when taken away,
Life isn't as we planned.

Sometimes you are the fisherman; sometimes, the chum.

GULLIBLE YOUTH

I smile
at gullible youth
and what
they have to say,

then find
myself thinking back,
I, too,
was once that way.

The more you talk the less you learn.

IN THE EYES

Words can play
A cruel game,
Of passion
And deceit.

But in the eyes,
All truth lies,
Whenever
They shall meet.

Ambiguity is the scoundrel's best defense;
circumlocution his most valuable ally.

ISN'T IT STRANGE

Isn't it strange
how we spend all our time
acquiring things
we don't need,

hoarding the insignificant
that binds us in our greed.

Through the selfishness
of grabbing,
we succumb without reason

like a plastic bell
that tries to ring,
we commit the utmost treason.

While multitudes of people starve
we dig a deeper hole,
in which we choose to cast away
the essence of our soul.

Everybody's doing it
so tell me, why shouldn't I,
to take what life has to beget
before I wither and die.

Yet all that I have strived for
and conspired here to save,
won't buy me a pauper's dream
once I'm past the grave.

The more you own, the more you are owned.

INSPIRATION

Inspiration
Rarely comes

When sitting
With paper and pen,

And by the time
You get it together

The thought
Won't come again.

It is too late to discuss the diameter of the fire hose when your house is burning down.

TO BORROW

It is wise
now to borrow,

you might not live
until tomorrow.

Plan for the future but don't bank on it.

JERUSALEM FIGHTS

All religions
killing each other
an eye for an eye,
no compromising.

Jerusalem fights
into the night,
a peaceful dawn,
never rising.

No one can hate with more passion than a religious zealot.

LEARN TO FORGET

The past
will give you
future regret,

if you cannot
finally
learn to forget.

Be mindful of the past but don't live
in it.

LIFE AND DEATH

Life and death
are one in the same,

mirroring each other
with different names,

transparent sisters
that laugh and cry,

obstinate brothers
that fight and die.

There is no such thing as one, big happy family.

LIKE A DIAMOND

Like a diamond
in the rough,

a cynic is a realist,
totally unbuffed.

I am not cynical enough to be optimistic.

LITTLE MEN

Little dogs
and little men,

bark and growl
time and again,

an innate desire
deep within,

to make those bigger
than them cower,

and genuflect
before their power.

A viper hisses when threatened.

MONARCHY AND THE COMMON PEOPLE

The illegitimate rule
of every monarchy
throughout the ragged course of time

depends entirely upon the inaction,
and benign cowardice,
of the common people.

For they are to blame
in helping their captors
by holding the shackles,

while their tormentors
fasten the ankle locks
firmly in place.

Once enchained,
the people feel it
to be their obligation,

to stand and wave flags,
adoring their oppressors,
and smile as they pass in review.

Fools are never without friends.

OF UNREQUITED PASSING

I trudge on,
my soul's lease
almost up,

yet I've found
no worthy standard
to which I can be proud of,

a useless charade,
the manacles of midnight
always with me,
the baggage of my past
a loathsome burden
of a bygone era,

tempting me with
the cadence of lies,
to build a hollow defense
of a lifetime squandered,

in the perplexity
of endless procrastination,
that sweet poison
wrapped in the essence
of the wild, white-flowered Oleander,

pure in appearance
yet deadly, once consumed,
in the symmetric richness,
of unrequited passing.

If you don't know where you are going,
any road will do.

WISHING WELL

Why is it that
in this society of ours,
even a wishing well
is based on the fact of money?

Some people go so far
as to think that, if a penny
can make a wish come true,
then a dime can do ten times better.

It is sad when I see people
who so tenaciously cling
to the misconception
that dreams can be bought
for any amount of money,

for those who adhere
to this line of thinking
will only find themselves
to be short-changed in the end.

Don't let anyone fool you; everybody
is a merchant.

OLD AGE

Old age is a cunning mammoth
that creeps up on you
with the lightning speed
of a cheetah,
    wearing sneakers
    in the night,
        ready to pounce
        at the break of day,
        just when you think
        everything is going your way.

I'm not afraid of death; it is the dying that bothers me.

THAT ULTIMATE VISIT

I am preoccupied with death.
Not on a morbid plane,
nor in a defeatist manner.

I simply consider death everyday.
For without death there would be
no life, no tape measure to determine time by,
no reason to set goals, no desire to succeed,
no value to love and hate, no point in living.

Death, in fact, doesn't mean it's all over.
In essence, it is living on a higher plane,
unencumbered by philosophers,
untainted by politics,
void of unfaithful friends.

Death is the first step into
the real unknown,
no job, no mortgage payments,
and no more taxes, an abyss unto itself.

Therefore, death should not be feared.
On the contrary, it aught to be
welcomed with open arms,
as it ultimately will embrace us all,
when it sees fit to pay that ultimate visit.

How you perceive the world outside is a direct reflection of what is going on inside.

OURSELVES

Treachery only flows
from the hearts of the beguiled,
the transgressed,
the wretched,
the rich, poor and defiled.

But more than all the above
it oozes from the pores
of the most heinous
of all purveyors,
seeping abundant
from evil iniquities,
the tainted souls
that we so piously refer to
as ourselves.

History does not repeat itself – people do.

PARENTAL GUIDANCE

Parents, not the children,
are to blame as to how the off-spring
behave, and how they act.
If a well-placed hand is not administered,
at the appropriate time, then children
have no boundaries on which to rely,
and invariably bounce off uncharted walls,
where rules do not exist, where anything goes,
where all is OK for the children,
but not for anyone else.

In this climate
of misconstrued, undisciplined, upbringing
the loving parents misinterpret
the concept of spare the rod
spoil the child,
to the inverted application of,
you must spoil the child
so spare the rod,
to the point where
parents, nowadays,
do not talk to their children,
they negotiate with them,
where the child commands
the center of attention,
and the parents are
the ones who meekly nod
their heads in resigned desperation.

Spank your son when he is young, so you don't have to beat him when he is older.

PATIENCE

If only I had
the patience of the stars,
to stand in silence
and watch as the universe
goes about its way,
not complaining
as to the way things are
nor wishing how
things aught to be,
instead, just existing
in muted observation
at all that surrounds me.

But then, what would
the essence of life mean,
seeing, but not acting,
being part of the audience
and not in the play itself,
a vicarious victim
of whimsical passivity,
the common element
of most mortal humans
pretending to be alive
yet in no way whatsoever
relevant in any sense of the word.

Freedom and security are mutually exclusive.

PENSION PIMP SUPREME

Be cautious, I was told, hold your tongue
when it wants to wag with indignation
against those who know better.

Don't set yourself up as a fool.
Rather, bide your time and strike
at the most opportune moment.

Be bold, yet cunning, cowardly, but brave,
smooth, yet coarse enough to be accepted
by the masses, as one of them.

Plead your case in the most eloquent of terms,
while remembering to talk straight
to the common people.

Conceal your utmost fears, yet, at the same time,
confessing to Original Sin.

For in doing so you will gain the confidence
of the working class, and be accepted within their ranks.

Be conservative in action, yet liberal in word and deed.
Curry favor from those in power but deny it to those in need.

Promise what you can't deliver
but retain a repository tone to do your utmost best.

Propagate faith but bear in mind you are a representative
of the Status Quo, and must always acquiesce to their wishes.

Don't overstep the limits of acceptability, that have been
set by others, for you, but present yourself as an outsider.

Dwell not on the plight of the invalid
but concede to be close to the cause.

Profess to feel for the hungry,
feign compassion for the less fortunate,
condolences to the poor, yet distance yourself
from direct contact therein.

Acquiesce to the pious, but extend yourself to the sinner,
while always binding your loyalty to the protection of the group.

Pin your hopes on the helpless
while in the shadows, tie your true bond
to the ribbons of the rich.

Extend your body to the needy, but secure your foundation
in the cement of the well-heeled, for therein lies your security.

Do all these things and you will become a permanent politician,
a pension pimp supreme, supping at the trough of public payment
with all goods and services accorded your standing in life,

while earning your keep on a daily basis,
speaking in convoluted tongues, a prostitute of the highest order,
while constantly bartering different parts of the whole.

Democracy is the petticoat of tyranny.

PEOPLE READ

People read
what they want to read
regardless of what's on the page,

and then they think
they read what's written
and fly into a rage.

They wail and flail
and gnash their teeth,
on misassumptions feed,

there's nothing sadder
than an educated man
who hasn't learned to read.

People only listen to what they want
to hear.

POETS AND ARTISTS

Most poets and artists
consider themselves
above the masses
of everyday citizenry

because they happen to have
a special knack for putting things
into words or pictures.

How much better are they
than the carpenter who builds
the poet's house,
or the garbage man
who collects the artist's trash?

If you talk down to people, they will never look up to you.

PROFESSORS

Theories and statistics
in them, the weak abide

content in Ivory Towers
afraid to go outside.

They footnote every thought
no original concept is there,

lacking courage to speak their mind
for them, they would not dare.

So on they go not seeking truth
nor wisdom do they care,

for tenure is their only thought
as thirsty students glare.

Good teachers get paid in smiles.

PROGRESSIVE MANKIND

The hungry treasury of confiscated minds,
clamored for more gold, an abundance of grain,
the willful donation of coagulated blood,
if nothing else was available.

Those who dared to think differently,
were summarily executed, to the gleeful delight
of the mass of ignorance now in command.

And the concept of the freedom of man
was vanquished with a fervor, in which the thunder
of the universe exposed itself in a show of naked jealously.

The horrid tranquility of passive acquiescence,
the grotesque cowardliness of sniveling sycophants
proclaiming to be only interested in the will of the people,

crawling in the shadows of militant peace-makers,
forging alliances of painless executions,
in the name of their conjured up god.

Least we live in the proximity of the heathen personified,
the community of the sublime iniquity,
fully reliant on the destitute of believers,

pleasure of passion revived, the death of the remote mind,
in favor of coordinated, communal thinking.

Yet truth, even in the darkness of the surrounding fold,
possesses the power to set men free, while fending off those
who would rather extinguish the light of freedom forever,
blinding those with deafening darkness,
who seek only justice for all who walk in stumble,
gated security, of constant mental deficiency,
forever in search of the right way to go.

Time is ripe to burn the books, pillage the fields
of those who work for a living, castigate the man
who tills the soil, make fun of the free-thinker,
vilify the believer of truth,
stamp out the whole lot with a vestige of
negative connotation, beguiled in lingering subservience,
while all the time pretending to be of the willful mob.

For in the pretense of the yoke of eternal bondage,
lies the excrement of personal security,
mired in a sense of ever-present guilt, woven in the marrow
of those who died before us, so as to make
the free decision to become, forever,
a slave of the New World Order,
in the Compliance of Progressive Mankind.

The minds of our children are too precious to entrust to any form of government education.

PROSTITUTES

More prostitutes lurk

In three-piece suits,

Than mini-skirts

And high-heeled boots.

Eloquence is the language of lies; the truth speaks for itself.

PAL

As I laid him on the doctor's table
guilt raged inside me, more so than the cancer
that had ravaged Pal's body for the last year.
It was time to end his misery, his muffled moans,
inability to walk, uncontrolled bowels, blood in his urine.

We had been together for 15 years
he, always at my side, smiling with his tail,
running after me, letting me win,
even though he could outpace me
anytime he wished to do so.

He never missed a chance to greet me at the door,
lay silently by my side after dinner, me with a Scotch in hand,
Pal content just to be together.

I had raised him from a puppy, took care of him
when he was sick, washed him in the bathtub,
splashing and nosing the bubbles
as I got just as wet trying to bathe him.

He never complained, lent a willing ear when I was down,
forever agreeing with my opinion, nodded his understanding,
yet all the while gave me comfort and support without being asked.

As the vet applied the injection, I started to cry, my hand caressing
Pal's face, instinctively him licking my hand one last time,
trying to make me feel better, reassuring me
that I was doing the right thing, eyes full of forgiveness,
in his undying faith that I would always be there to take care of him.

Unlike man, a dog will never bite the hand that feeds him.

A SUNNY DAY

Everyday
starts with
a ray of hope,
a glimmer of
the new,
a revitalized self
looking for
a better path
that leads
to a brighter
tomorrow.
Think positive,
even through
the aches and pains
that drain vital energy
from your soul,
negative thoughts
that seem to plague us all
into thinking,
what's the use of it all.
Instead, keep moving forward,
looking in all directions
for that sliver of brightness,
and smile when you find it
embracing your face
in unbounded excitement.
And, whatever you do,
never close the blinds
on a sunny day.

I do, because I will.